The Site of Memory

The Site of Memory

TONI MORRISON

Published in 2025 by Spiral House, an imprint of Silver Press.

'The Site of Memory' by Toni Morrison was first published in
Inventing the Truth, edited by William Zinsser, 1995.

ISBN-13: 978-1-0685918-9-1

Design by Rose Nordin
Cover image by Mark Lowe
Typeset in Adobe Caslon Pro by Alice Spawls
Printed and bound in the UK by CPI

EU GPSR Authorised Representative: Logos Europe,
9 rue Nicolas Poussin, 17000, La Rochelle, France.
contact@logoseurope.eu

1 3 5 7 9 10 8 6 4 2

My inclusion in a series of talks on autobiography and memoir is not entirely a misalliance. Although it's probably true that a fiction writer thinks of his or her work as alien in that company, what I have to say may suggest why I'm not completely out of place here. For one thing, I might throw into relief the differences between self-recollection (memoir) and fiction, and also some of the similarities – the places where those two crafts embrace and where that embrace is symbiotic.

But the authenticity of my presence here lies in the fact that a very large part of my own literary heritage is the autobiography. In this country, the print origins of black literature (as distinguished from the oral origins) were slave narratives. These book-length narratives (autobiographies, recollections, memoirs), of which well over a hundred were published, are familiar texts to historians and students of black history. They range from the adventure-packed life of Olaudah Equiano's *The Interesting Narrative of the Life of Olaudah Equiano, or Gustavus Vassa, the African, Written by Himself* (1769) to the quiet desperation of *Incidents in the Life of a Slave Girl: Written by Herself* (1861), in which Harriet Jacob ('Linda Brent') records hiding for seven years in a room too small to stand up in; from the political savvy of Frederick Douglass's *Narrative of the Life of Frederick Douglass, an American Slave, Written by Himself* (1849) to the subtlety and modesty of Henry Bibb, whose voice, in *Life and Adventures of Henry Bibb, an American Slave, Written by Himself* (1849), is surrounded by ('loaded with' is a better phrase) documents attesting to its authenticity. Bibb is careful to note that his formal schooling (three weeks) was short, but that he was 'educated in the school of adversity, whips and chains'. Born in Kentucky, he put aside his plans to escape in order to marry. But when he learned that he was the father of a slave and watched the degradation of his wife and child, he reactivated those plans.

Whatever the style and circumstances of these narratives, they were written to say principally two things. One:

'This is my historical life – my singular, special example that is personal, but that also represents the race.' Two: 'I write this text to persuade other people – you, the reader, who is probably not black – that we are human beings worthy of God's grace and the immediate abandonment of slavery.' With these two missions in mind, the narratives were clearly pointed.

In Equiano's account, the purpose is quite upfront. Born in 1745 near the Niger River and captured at the age of ten, he survived the Middle Passage, American plantation slavery, wars in Canada and the Mediterranean, learned navigation and clerking from a Quaker named Robert King, and bought his freedom at twenty-one. He lived as a free servant, travelling widely and living most of his latter life in England. Here he is speaking to the British without equivocation: 'I hope to have the satisfaction of seeing the renovation of liberty and justice resting on the British government . . . I hope and expect the attention of gentlemen of power . . . May the time come – at least the speculation is to me pleasing – when the sable people shall gratefully commemorate the auspicious era of extensive freedom.' With typically eighteenth-century reticence he records his singular and representative life for one purpose: to change things. In fact, he and his co-authors did change things. Their works gave fuel to the fires that abolitionists were setting everywhere.

More difficult was getting the fair appraisal of literary critics. The writings of church martyrs and confessors are and were read for the eloquence of their message as well as their experience of redemption, but the American slaves' autobiographical narratives were frequently scorned as 'biased', 'inflammatory' and 'improbable'. These attacks are particularly difficult to understand in view of the fact that it was extremely important, as you can imagine, for the writers of these narratives to appear as objective as possible – not to offend the reader by being too angry, or by showing too much outrage, or by calling the reader names. As recently as 1966, Paul Edwards, who edited and abridged Equiano's story, praises the narrative for its refusal to be 'inflammatory'. 'As a rule', Edwards writes,

> 'he [Equiano] puts no emotional pressure on the reader other than that which the situation itself contains – his language does not strain after our sympathy, but expects it to be given naturally and at the proper time. This quiet avoidance of emotional display produces many of the best passages in the book.

Similarly, an 1836 review of Charles Bell's *Life and Adventures of a Fugitive Slave*, which appeared in *The*

Quarterly Anti-Slavery Magazine, praised Bell's account for its objectivity. 'We rejoice in the book the more, because it is not a partisan work ... It broaches no theory in regard to [slavery], nor proposes any mode or time of emancipation.'

As determined as these black writers were to persuade the reader of the evil of slavery, they also complimented him by assuming his nobility of heart and his high-mindedness. They tried to summon up his finer nature in order to encourage him to employ it. They knew that their readers were the people who could make a difference in terminating slavery. Their stories – of brutality, adversity and deliverance – had great popularity in spite of critical hostility in many quarters and patronising sympathy in others. There was a time when the hunger for 'slave stories' was difficult to quiet, as sales figures show. Douglass's *Narrative* sold 5,000 copies in four months; by 1847 it had sold 11,000 copies. Equiano's book had thirty-six editions between 1789 and 1850. Moses Roper's book had ten editions from 1837 to 1856; William Wells Brown's was reprinted four times in its first year. Solomon Northrop's book sold 27,000 copies before two years had passed. A book by Josiah Henson (argued by some to be the model for the 'Tom' of Harriet Beecher Stowe's *Uncle Tom's Cabin*) had a pre-publication sale of 5,000.

In addition to using their own lives to expose the horrors of slavery, they had a companion motive for their efforts. The prohibition against teaching a slave to read and write (which in many Southern states carried severe punishment) had to be scuttled at all costs. These writers knew that literacy was power. Voting, after all, was inextricably connected to the ability to read; literacy was a way of assuming and proving the 'humanity' that the Constitution denied them. That is why the narratives carry the subtitle 'written by himself' or 'herself', and include introductions and prefaces by white sympathisers to authenticate them. Other narratives, 'edited by' such well-known anti-slavery figures as Lydia Maria Child and John Greenleaf Whittier, contain prefaces to assure the reader how little editing was needed. A literate slave was supposed to be a contradiction in terms.

One has to remember that the climate in which they wrote reflected not only the Age of Enlightenment but its twin, born at the same time, the Age of Scientific Racism. David Hume, Immanuel Kant and Thomas Jefferson, to mention only a few, had documented their conclusions that blacks were incapable of intelligence. Frederick Douglass knew otherwise, and he wrote refutations of what Jefferson said in 'Notes on the State of Virginia': 'Never yet could I find that a black had uttered a thought above the level of plain narration, never see even an elementary trait of painting or sculpture' – a sentence that I have always thought ought to be engraved at the door to the Rockefeller Collection of African Art. Hegel, in 1813, had said that Africans had no 'history' and couldn't write in modern languages. Kant disregarded a perceptive observation by a black man by saying, 'This fellow was quite black from head to foot, a clear proof that what he said was stupid.'

Yet no slave society in the history of the world wrote more – or more thoughtfully – about its own enslavement. The milieu, however, dictated the purpose and the style. The narratives are instructive, moral and obviously representative. Some of them are patterned after the sentimental novel that was in vogue at the time. But whatever the level of eloquence or the form, popular taste discouraged the writers from dwelling too long or too carefully on the more sordid details of their experience. Whenever there was an unusually violent incident, or a scatological one, or something 'excessive', one finds the writer taking refuge in the literary conventions of the day. 'I was left in a state of distraction not to be described' (Equiano). 'But let us now leave the rough usage of the field . . . and turn our attention to the less repulsive slave life as it existed in the house of my childhood' (Douglass). 'I am not about to harrow the feelings of my readers by a terrific representation of the untold horrors of that fearful system of oppression. . . It is not my purpose to descend deeply into the dark and noisome caverns of the hell of slavery' (Henry Box Brown).

Over and over, the writers pull the narrative up short with a phrase such as, 'But let us drop a veil over these proceedings too terrible to relate.' In shaping the experience to make it palatable to those who were in a position to alleviate it, they were silent about many things, and they 'forgot' many other things. There was a careful selection of the instances that they would record and a careful rendering of those that they chose to describe. Lydia Maria Child identified the problem in her introduction to 'Linda Brent's' tale of sexual abuse:

> I am well aware that many will accuse me of indecorum for presenting these pages to the public; for the experiences of this intelligent and much-injured woman belong to a class which some call delicate subjects, and others indelicate. This peculiar phase of Slavery has generally been kept veiled; but the public ought to be made acquainted with its monstrous features, and I am willing to take the responsibility of presenting them with the veil drawn [aside].

But most important – at least for me – there was no mention of their interior life.

For me – a writer in the last quarter of the twentieth century, not much more than a hundred years after Emancipation, a writer who is black and a woman – the exercise is very different. My job becomes how to rip that veil drawn over 'proceedings too terrible to relate'. The exercise is also critical for any person who is black, or who belongs to any marginalised category, for, historically, we were seldom invited to participate in the discourse, even when we were its topic.

Moving that veil aside requires, therefore, certain things. First of all, I must trust my own recollections. I must also depend on the recollections of others. Thus memory weighs heavily in what I write, in how I begin and in what I find to be significant. Zora Neale Hurston said, 'Like the dead seeming cold rocks, I have memories within that came out of the material that went to make me.' These 'memories within' are the subsoil of my work. But memories and recollections won't give me total access to the unwritten interior life of these people. Only the act of the imagination can help me.

If writing is thinking and discovery and selection and order and meaning, it is also awe and reverence and mystery and magic. I suppose I could dispense with the last four if I were not so deadly serious about fidelity to the milieu out of which I write and in which my ancestors actually lived. Infidelity to that milieu – the absence of the interior life, the deliberate excising of it from the records that the slaves themselves told – is precisely the problem in the discourse that proceeded without us. How I gain access to that interior life is what drives me and is the part of this talk which both distinguishes my fiction from autobiographical strategies and which also embraces certain autobiographical strategies. It's a kind of literary archaeology: on the basis of some information and a little bit of guesswork you journey to a site to see what remains were left behind and to reconstruct the world that these remains imply. What makes it fiction is the nature of the imaginative act: my reliance on the image – on the remains – in addition to recollection, to yield up a kind of a truth. By 'image', of course, I don't mean 'symbol'; I simply mean 'picture' and the feelings that accompany the picture.

Fiction, by definition, is distinct from fact. Presumably it's the product of imagination – invention – and it claims the freedom to dispense with 'what really happened', or where it really happened, or when it really happened, and nothing in it needs to be publicly verifiable, although much in it can be verified. By contrast, the scholarship of the biographer and the literary critic seems to us only trustworthy when the events of fiction can be traced to some publicly verifiable fact. It's the research of the 'Oh, yes, this is where he or she got it from' school, which gets its own credibility from excavating the credibility of the sources of the imagination, not the nature of the imagination.

The work that I do frequently falls, in the minds of most people, into that realm of fiction called fantastic, or mythic, or magical, or unbelievable. I'm not comfortable with these labels. I consider that my single gravest responsibility (in spite of that magic) is not to lie. When I hear someone say, 'Truth is stranger than fiction', I think that old chestnut is truer than we know, because it doesn't say that truth is truer than fiction; just that it's stranger, meaning that it's odd. It may be excessive, it may be more interesting, but the important thing is that it's random – and fiction is not random. Therefore the crucial distinction for me is not the difference between fact and fiction, but the distinction between fact and truth. Because facts can exist without human intelligence, but truth cannot. So if I'm looking to find and expose a truth about the interior life of people who didn't write it (which doesn't mean that they didn't have it); if I'm trying to fill in the blanks that the slave narratives left – to part the veil that was so frequently drawn, to implement the stories that I heard – then the approach that's most productive and most trustworthy for me is the recollection that moves from the image to the text. Not from the text to the image.

Simone de Beauvoir, in *A Very Easy Death*, says, 'I don't know why I was so shocked by my mother's death.' When she heard her mother's name being called at the funeral by the priest, she says,

> Emotion seized me by the throat . . . 'Françoise de Beauvoir'; the words brought her to life; they summed up her history, from birth to marriage to widowhood to the grave. Françoise de Beauvoir – that retiring woman, so rarely named, became an important person.

The book becomes an exploration both into her own grief and into the images in which the grief lay buried.

Unlike Mme. de Beauvoir, Frederick Douglass asks the reader's patience for spending about half a page on the death of his grandmother – easily the most profound loss he had suffered – and he apologises by saying, in effect, 'It really was very important to me. I hope you aren't bored by my indulgence.' He makes no attempt to explore that death: its images or its meaning. His narrative is as close to factual as he can make it, which leaves no room for subjective speculation. James Baldwin, on the other hand, in *Notes of a Native Son*, says, in recording his father's life and his own relationship to his father, 'All of my father's Biblical texts and songs, which I had decided were meaningless, were ranged before me at his death like empty bottles, waiting to hold the meaning which life would give them for me.' And then his text fills those bottles. Like Simone de Beauvoir, he moves from the event to the image that it left. My route is the reverse: The image comes first and tells me what the 'memory' is about.

I can't tell you how I felt when my father died. But I was able to write *Song of Solomon* and imagine, not him, and not his specific interior life, but the world that he inhabited and the private or interior life of the people in it. And I can't tell you how I felt reading to my grandmother while she was turning over and over in her bed (because she was dying, and she was not comfortable), but I could try to reconstruct the world that she lived in. And I have suspected, more often than not, that I *know* more than she did, that I *know* more than my grandfather and my great-grandmother did, but I also know that I'm no wiser than they were. And whenever I have tried earnestly to diminish their vision and prove to myself that I know more, and when I have tried to speculate on their interior life and match it up with my own, I have been overwhelmed every time by the richness of theirs compared to my own. Like Frederick Douglass talking about his grandmother, and James Baldwin talking about his father, and Simone de Beauvoir talking about her mother, these people are my access to me: they are my entrance into my own interior life. Which is why the images that float around them, the remains, so to speak, at the archeological site – surface first, and they surface so vividly and so compellingly that I acknowledge them as my route to a reconstruction of a world, to an exploration of an interior life that was not written and to the revelation of a kind of truth.

So the nature of my research begins with something as ineffable and as flexible as a dimly recalled figure, the corner of a room, a voice. I began to write my second book, which was called *Sula*, because of my preoccupation with a picture of a woman and the way in which I heard her name pronounced. Her name was Hannah, and I think she was a friend of my mother's. I don't remember seeing her very much, but what I do remember is the colour around her – a kind of violet, a suffusion of something violet – and her eyes, which appeared to be half closed. But what I remember most is how the women said her name: how they said 'Hannah Peace' and smiled to themselves, and there was some secret about her that they knew, which they didn't talk about, at least not in my hearing, but it seemed *loaded* in the way in which they said her name. And I suspected that she was a little bit of an outlaw but that they approved in some way.

And then, thinking about their relationship to her and the way in which they talked about her, the way in which they articulated her name, made me think about friendship between women. What is it that they forgive each other for? And what it is that is unforgivable in the world of women. I don't want to know any more about Miss Hannah Peace, and I'm not going to ask my mother who she really was and what did she do and what were you laughing about and why were you smiling? Because my experience when I do this with my mother is so crushing: She will give you *the* most pedestrian information you ever heard, and I would like to keep all of my remains and my images intact in their mystery when I begin. Later I will get to the facts. That way I can explore two worlds – the actual and the possible.

What I want to do in this talk is to track an image from picture to meaning to text – a journey which appears in the novel that I'm writing now, which is called *Beloved.* I'm trying to write a particular kind of scene, and I see corn on the cob. To 'see' corn on the cob doesn't mean that it suddenly hovers; it only means that it keeps coming back. And in trying to figure out 'What is all this corn doing?' I discover what it *is* doing.

I see the house where I grew up in Lorain, Ohio. My parents had a garden some distance away from our house, and they didn't welcome me and my sister there, when we were young, because we were not able to distinguish between the things that they wanted to grow and the things that they didn't, so we were not able to hoe, or weed, until much later.

I see them walking, together, away from me. I'm looking at their backs and what they're carrying in their arms: their tools, and maybe a peck basket. Sometimes when they walk away from me they hold hands, and they go to this other place in the garden. They have to cross some railroad tracks to get there.

I also am aware that my mother and father sleep at odd hours because my father works many jobs and works at night. And these naps are times of pleasure for me and my sister because nobody's giving us chores, or telling us what to do, or nagging us in any way. In addition to which, there is some feeling of pleasure in them that I'm only vaguely aware of. They're very rested when they take these naps. And later on in the summer we have an opportunity to eat corn, which is the one plant that I can distinguish from the others, and which is the harvest that I like the best; the others are the food that no child likes – the collards, the okra, the strong, violent vegetables that I would give a great deal for now. But I do like the corn because it's sweet, and because we all sit down to eat it, and it's finger food, and it's hot, and it's even good cold, and there are neighbours in, and there are uncles in, and it's easy, and it's nice.

The picture of the corn and the nimbus of emotion surrounding it became a powerful one in the manuscript I'm now completing.

Authors arrive at text and subtext in thousands of ways, learning each time they begin anew how to recognise a valuable idea and how to render the texture that accompanies, reveals or displays it to its best advantage. The process by which this is accomplished is endlessly fascinating to me. I have always thought that as an editor for twenty years I understood writers better than their most careful critics, because in examining the manuscript in each of its subsequent stages I knew the author's process, how his or her mind worked, what was effortless, what took time, where the 'solution' to a problem came from. The end result – the book – was all that the critic had to go on.

Still, for me, that was the least important aspect of the work. Because, no matter how 'fictional' the account of these writers, or how much it was a product of invention, the act of imagination is bound up with memory. You know, they straightened out the Mississippi River in places, to make room for houses and livable acreage. Occasionally the river floods these places. 'Floods' is the word they use, but in fact it is not flooding; it is remembering. Remembering where it used to be. All water has a perfect memory and is forever trying to get back to where it was. Writers are like that: remembering where we were, what valley we ran through, what the banks were like, the light that was there and the route back to our original place. It is emotional memory - what the nerves and the skin remember as well as how it appeared. And a rush of imagination is our 'flooding'.

Along with personal recollection, the matrix of the work I do is the wish to extend, fill in and complement slave autobiographical narratives. But only the matrix. What comes of all that is dictated by other concerns, not least among them the novel's own integrity. Still, like water, I remember where I was before I was 'straightened out'.

*

Q. I would like to ask about your point of view as a novelist. Is it a vision, or are you taking the part of the particular characters?

I try sometimes to have genuinely minor characters just walk through, like a walk-on actor. But I get easily distracted by them, because a novelist's imagination goes like that: Every little road looks to me like an adventure, and once you begin to claim it and describe it, it looks like more, and you invent more and more and more. I don't mind doing that in my first draft, but afterward I have to cut back. I have seen myself get distracted, and people have loomed much larger than I had planned, and minor characters have seemed a little bit more interesting than they need to be for the purposes of the book. In that case I try to endow them: if there are little pieces of information that I want to reveal, I let them do some of the work. But I try not to get carried away; I try to restrain it, so that, finally, the texture is consistent and nothing is wasted; there are no words in the final text that are unnecessary, and no people who are not absolutely necessary.

As for the point of view, there should be the illusion that it's the characters' point of view, when in fact it isn't; it's really the narrator who is there but who doesn't make herself (in my case) known in that role. I like the feeling of a told story, where you hear a voice but you can't identify it, and you think it's your own voice. It's a comfortable voice, and it's a guiding voice, and it's alarmed by the same things that the reader is alarmed by, and it doesn't know what's going to happen next either. So you have this sort of guide. But that guide can't have a personality; it can only have a sound, and you have to feel comfortable with this voice, and then this voice can easily abandon itself and reveal the interior dialogue of a character. So it's a combination of using the point of view of various characters but still retaining the power to slide in and out, provided that when I'm 'out' the reader doesn't see little fingers pointing to what's in the text.

What I really want is that intimacy in which the reader is under the impression that he isn't really reading this; that he is participating in it as he goes along. It's unfolding, and he's always two beats ahead of the characters and right on target.

Q. You have said that writing is a solitary activity. Do you go into steady seclusion when you're writing, so that your feelings are sort of contained, or do you have to get away, and go out shopping and . . . ?

I do all of it. I've been at this book for three years. I go out shopping, and I stare, and I do whatever. It goes away. Sometimes it's very intense and I walk – I mean, I write a sentence and I jump up and run outside or something; it sort of beats you up. And sometimes I don't. Sometimes I write long hours every day. I get up at 5:30 am and just go do it, and if I don't like it the next day, I throw it away. But I sit down and do it. By now I know how to get to that place where something is working. I didn't always know: I thought every thought I had was interesting – because it was mine. Now I know better how to throw away things that are not useful. I can stand around and do other things and think about it at the same time. I don't mind not writing every minute; I'm not so terrified.

When you first start writing – and I think it's true for a lot of beginning writers – you're scared to death that if you don't get that sentence right that minute, it's never going to show up again. And it isn't. But it doesn't matter – another one will, and it'll probably be better. And I don't mind writing badly for a couple of days because I know I can fix it – and fix it again and again and again, and it will be better. I don't have the hysteria that used to accompany some of those dazzling passages that I thought the world was just dying for me to remember. I'm a little more sanguine about it now. Because the best part of it all, the absolutely most delicious part, is finishing it and then doing it over. That's the thrill of a lifetime for me: if I can just get done with that first phase and then have infinite time to fix it and change it. I rewrite a lot, over and over again, so that it looks like I never did. I try to make it look like I never touched it, and that takes a lot of time and a lot of sweat.

Q. In *Song of Solomon,* what was the relationship between your memories and what you made up? Was it very tenuous?

Yes, it was tenuous. For the first time I was writing a book in which the central stage was occupied by men, and which had something to do with my loss, or my perception of loss, of a man (my father) and the world that disappeared with him. (It didn't, but I felt that it did.) So I was re-creating a time period that was his – not biographically his life or anything in it, I use whatever's around. But it seemed to me that there was this big void after he died, and I filled it with a book that was about men because my two previous books had had women as the central characters. So in that sense it was about my memories and the need to invent. I had to do something. I was in such a rage because my father was dead. The connections between us were threads that I either mined for a lot of strength or they were purely invention. But I created a male world and inhabited it and it had this quest – a journey from stupidity to epiphany, of a man, a complete man. It was my way of exploring all that, of trying to figure out what he may have known.